How To Gain Friends and Influence People

The Art of Social Interaction

Table of Contents

Introduction 1

Chapter 1: The Art Of Persuasion 4

Chapter 2: Being Charismatic In The Presence Of Others 15

Chapter 3: How To Gain Friends and Win People Over 25

Chapter 4: How To Have Social Confidence 32

Chapter 5: Your Friends Are A Goldmine For You 38

Chapter 6: Using Your Talents And Abilities 46

Chapter 7: How To Love Yourself First 51

Chapter 8: Being Of Influence To Others In A Positive Way ... 59

Chapter 9: The Art Of Social Interaction 68

Chapter 10: Being Perseverant As An Influential Person 76

Introduction

The art of persuasion exists inside of all of us, and we live and learn from the concepts that we go through and the experiences that we're a part of. Many of us out there seek to have persuasive and influential abilities to gain what we want out of life, though these abilities should be used mostly to do good work for others, help others change their life and to do good for the greater good of humanity. What is persuasion? Persuasion is a technique that most people use along with energy and charisma to become enveloped in the concept of social interaction and to be able to have greater social skills and to be of a great influence to others.

Would you like to win friends over and have influence over others? Are you an articulate person and speaker or are you more socially anxious or shy? In order to be the kind of person who is able to make friends in this world you will need to be articulate, intelligent and exude an air of confidence and finesse. You will want to be the person that everyone wants to be around, and the person who people really aren't inside themselves. Being an influential person means possessing gifts, talents, charisma and abilities that most people just don't normally have and being an exceptional person. However, not everyone is going to be exceptional, so you may have to improvise and just appear to be the exceptional person you might aim to be but may not be as of yet.

The art of persuasion is a gift and talent that someone can use to harness their personal social power and different aspects of charisma within themselves in order to use specific gifts to be able to sway people into believing or thinking what they want them to believe or think. To be a persuasive person takes skill, ability, and a gift that can be natural or developed. Getting more friends in life and more people to like you or enjoy your company means you'll need to be likeable, attractive, have a good personality and be very friendly towards people. These are just a few of the key methods to gaining more great friendships in your life and getting more out of what you want in your current reality.

Have you ever wanted to be of influence to others and gain more friends and more positive supportive people in your life? You can do this by becoming a very likeable person who possesses an abundance of wonderful, beautiful charisma and you can become an overall better person socially. Gaining a great amount of social confidence can assist you with improving your social interactions and allowing you to gain some stability within yourself and let you be the person that people want to be around and the person that people want to be friends with.

Chapter 1

THE ART OF PERSUASION

The Art of Persuasion

Persuasion is a technique and art that a person needs to know and understand in order to be able to receive the things they want and need in life. In order to be an influential and persuasive person in this world socially and in other ways, you will need to be articulate, intelligent, a great speaker and possess social confidence. The art of persuasion is the ability to convince people to agree with you without using force, manipulation, or deception. It's a skill that can be improved through study and practice.

It involves using communication techniques to influence other people's attitudes, beliefs, thoughts or actions. It acts upon building credibility, knowing a person's audience, appealing to emotions and presenting logical arguments. Persuasion is in fact a negotiation and learning process through which a person leads people to a problem's solution. It involves the framing of arguments, an effective presentation of supporting evidence, and finding the right emotional feelings with your audience and those who you're attempting to persuade.

Persuasion is a technique that is used diligently by those who seek to live in a world where they exist solely to gain benefit by convincing others of what they believe in though it should be done through the lens of moral means. Persuasion is a unique method used by those who harness and fully understand the concept of social finesse, confidence, and other social arts in order to be able to utilize these techniques to gain the responses they need for their own selves. People often feel as if persuasion is something akin to a sales technique, but it supercedes that of a sales tactic that people may use and yet does not involve any form of deception.

The art of persuasion is a method that people use in order to assist themselves and others and influence their lives through means of convincing others of what they truly want others to believe or feel. Persuasive techniques can be used to manipulate and influence others into believing what you seek them to believe yet should be done under the guise of moral and decent means, not deceitful, negative or abusive methods.

The art of persuasion is a beautiful technique used in order to be able to showcase your abilities to others in order to further develop your persuasive talents and be able to manipulate others into believing and doing what you want them to do and to gain from them that you may need. It however should only be used to benefit others in a positive and beneficial way and not for your own personal gain or used to negatively manipulate or influence people in order to gain what you need from them.

It is the social confidence and ability to be able to utilize along with your own energies in order to receive what you need out of someone. it can be used in many facets and ways, including jobs sales positions, business dealings, relationships, and it can be a great benefit to you if you're able to utilize in the most effective way.

As a persuasive person, you're seeking to change the way people think about themselves, their lives, their jobs, their habits but doing so in a very positive and influential way. You can change people's lives and how they perceive themselves, their situations, and any aspect about themselves. You're going to want to help them change their perspective on anything negative in their world and make it a very positive, beneficial and beautiful one. You can be a persuasive person as a life coach, teacher, healer, or in any field or profession you desire to be a part of.

How can I be a more persuasive person

Persuasion takes confidence yet most people may not understand that this is not utilized in a negative connotation or context. It takes charisma, energy style grace, and many other qualities in order to be able to possess and master the art of being a persuasive and manipulative person in a positive way in order to gain the things that you might want out of life.

The art of persuasion is the action by which a person exists in a world of enhancing their life by incorporating others into it and using their social skills in a charismatic and beneficial way to gain what they need out of a situation.

It's important to live a life of goodness and morality. We don't want to live in a world where we're out to get what we want only for ourselves. We should be living lives of utmost morality, and in worlds of wanting to do better for those close to us and for people in general. It is of importance that we do not use our talents, gifts and social abilities that we harnessed and develop our gain or manipulate or influence people through deception or malicious means.

Persuasive techniques can often be used to gain benefit solely for a person for selfish reasons and this is something that should be frowned upon. So how do we live in this world and get friends that we want in like and who want to be around us and how can we influence people into liking us and being the center of attention and someone who was wanted by others?

In order to live in this world and be successful, we need to enhance our lives and grant us blessings that encompass positive ideations and goodness that we spread to those around us, rather than seeking to manipulate others to receive what we so desire.

Are you a persuasive person or do people not tend to believe in the things that you say or the ideas that you bring to the table? Being a persuasive person takes technique, skill, grace, eloquence and a host of other abilities and talents that a person will need to utilize in order to be able to bring their influential nature into fruition.

You are a gracious, wonderful, influential person who has these hidden talents and abilities that you may not know of and have the capability of using them if you so choose to utilize them. Utilizing them doesn't mean doing harm to others or using them in a negative format, but moreso, using them in a beneficial, fun, and positive way to help or benefit others in a good way and even to get the little things that you so want and desire.

Living in a world full of chaos and deception

We live in a world of chaos and deception. Negativity surrounds us and people get caught up in a world of selfishness and greed, and becoming in this state of mind. Evil encompasses many people in generations out there, and people are in a state of being confused and lacking in general morality. It's easy to envelope in the world and generation that we live in. Evil sometimes even becomes cool to some and people live in a general state of lack of awareness of their own selves and behaviors. It's important to stay true to yourself and live by the morals you've always held near and dear to you, and to always fulfill your own needs as well as the needs of others. You'll want to live by the standards that were taught to you hopefully and albeit as long as they uphold the moral code of the world and society. The moral code is the standards by which people uphold the morals of everyday living and life. It is the most important code that people should live by, and people need to abide by these rules in order to live in a better and more organized and fulfilled world and society.

Sometimes, it can be difficult to live by this moral code, because people have strayed from their belief systems and have forgotten what they truly believe in or how they feel about the world and decide to just live on a whim or by standards that are far lesser, which include, greed, selfishness, evil, pride, lust and arrogance. People end up living in a reality of chaos and deception and rarely care about the consequences that it has on others or what it can do to their life or how it affects their life. Committing treasonous negative acts in life can create havoc in the world and in life and can create negative outcomes for a person, increase negative karma in this life, generate an abundance of negative energy rather than positive energy, and is a very bad idea for people in general.

As positive and successful people, we want to stay away from the common role that we live in and move further towards a land and in a world that is intertwined with hope morality and good natures beliefs and ideations. We should be seeking to strive to live in goodness and blessings and love rather than selfishness monetary gain and pride. You'll want to live in a world full of positive blessings and ideals where you commit good and have good intentions towards others, so that you'll harvest and create more positive energies and good karmic energies in your life and world. You'll also spread these thoughtforms and energies out into the universe so that more positivity can come back to you in general, rather than negative or challenging outcomes.

What kind of world do you exist in? Were you raised with love, happiness, and joy or with narcissism arrogance and pride? What is normal to you? Positivity, success and greatness come with hard work, dedication, talent and diligence with vanity, pride, prejudice, evil, and other negative connotations that exist in this world and on this planet. Were you taught the correct morals by your parents or during your upbringing? If you were, then hopefully you'll abide by those rules and regulations and live a life of morality and goodness, rather than one of selfishness and other forms of greed or evil.

How should we exist and live our lives?

We should be living our lives to the lens of positivity, love light, and goodness and not through the lens of cruelty evil or injustice. There is an abundance of injustice and evil in this world. This is the manner and method by which we need to stray away from constantly. Living to stop injustices that occur from happening should be our aim in life.

Many people seek to be happy, yet they live in a world where they're unable to encompass or grasp the concept of happiness. People have no knowledge or concept of what happiness is or have ever existed in the specific state in reality at all. Many people live in a world of negativity where they're constantly down on themselves or putting themselves down or others around them. It is of utmost importance to leave this state of mind and way of thinking if you're fathoming becoming a confident successful and influential leader and person in your life.

Happiness is a blessing that many people may seek but most don't generally think about. They seek to feel the bliss energy incumbent within the processes of being happy and fulfilled and joyous within yet they have no clue or knowledge of how to go about doing this and rarely think about it on a regular basis.

People have become ingrained in the world that they currently live in which may consist of extreme amounts of negativity, anger, depression, mental issues and stress along with other negative situations. In order to learn study and master the concept of influence persuasion and be able to get what you want out of life and be the success that you so desire you will need to master the art of possessing internal happiness and success within your mind life and world and achieving internal bliss first before you can gain the approval of others and of the world that you intently seek and desire.

Beauty as the benefactor of our existence

Many people seek to become engrossed in the concept of beauty

The concept of beauty exists in this world as the sole beneficiary of many people's lives, loves, and mental states. People become obsessed with the concept of beauty, and they seek deep within themselves to emulate or be a part of that which is beautiful encapsulated or special. Beauty is a deep-rooted enthralling concept that humanity is brainwashed into worshipping and although it can be pleasurable or pleasing in some forms, it is not a necessity to others, although people seem to flock to it and find good reason to want to become a part of it or adore it.

Although beauty can be an amazing concept and extremely enthralling, it is something that we should not chase after or seek to be a part of solely for the concept of beauty can become the down spiraling and dwindling of many people's lives and souls.

The beauty that people so seek and chase after is not the motor method of beauty that people should be looking for. There are aspects of beauty that we should become enthralled with and should strive to be a part of. These concepts include the beauty of nature, goodness, love, the gift of light and imagination, and the goodness present within each and every living being to exist.

The concept of passion

The art of passion exists within all of us. We all should seek to live our lives within the lens of beauty love compassion generosity and security. Passion exists as a gateway to let us encompass our secret wants and desires and become ingrained with amazing notions and yearnings deep within us. We have deep feelings about our desires and beliefs and seek to share that with others or influence others into believing how we feel deep within.

Passion is the beauty and desire we so seek deep within our very core and souls. we yearn to exist in a state of consciousness and wonder where our innermost desires and beliefs reside. Love is the essence of the passion that resides within us, and we should seek to fulfill its very purpose by being a part of the love that exists within us.

Our passions and desires are of major importance in this world, and we need to harness them in the most delightful manner in order to become the internally happy creations we are meant to be and in order to skyrocket our successes and true confidence within and be greatness in many forms.

Passion is the key to harnessing our internal natures and inspiring our true selves within and allows us to express ourselves using our wonderful gifts and abilities and showcase ourselves to others through a lens of amazement and people perceiving us as someone amazing or great.

Being a passionate person means existing in a truthful and beautiful, wonderful nature of being happy and thrilled even flamboyant about your beliefs, truths, ideals and desires, and means getting excited over these concepts and aspects. Your passions and desires matter to the world and to you and you have every right to showcase them to others and use them for the benefit of yourself and of others. Passion exists to be the level of enthrallment for many people out there and allows the goodness and desire of others to seep forth into a humble, kind, decent, excited soul that is thrilled to share her experiences and joys with others.

Chapter 2

BEING CHARISMATIC IN THE PRESENCE OF OTHERS

Charisma is the key to social confidence

Your charisma is extremely unique to you, and it is the signature by which you actually speak to others through your energy, your own unique, interpersonal power and your own beautiful words. There is a way in art of being able to use your social skills and put together those abilities along with your energetic abilities, and your charisma in order to produce a masterful means of being able to communicate with others and influence others using these specific techniques. Being charismatic is of great importance when it comes to having the desire to influence others in life and work and within your relationships.

Being charismatic is something that not every person possesses however, there are many out there that desire to possess a very specific and special type of charisma that others simply do not have the qualities to utilize.

Charisma comes from within us. We all may seek to be charismatic people yet do not have what it takes to possess this specific kind of characteristic. Charisma is a personal quality that makes someone psychologically compelling and influential to others. It can be seen in how someone speaks, what they say, and how they look.

Charisma includes personal appeal, personal magnetism, attractiveness, sexual allure, and interest. It is about being able to exude outwardly the social graces and beauty that you so hold deep within and allowing yourself to become a wonderful and powerful influential person and soul towards others in the world and society.

In some fields, charisma is a type of leadership. Charismatic leaders can help their listeners understand, relate to, and remember their message.

Charisma is the manner and method by which a person displays their personal charm to others and their influence and personal beauty and energy. It is an important aspect of a person that exists to serve their social needs and allows them to present themselves to be a particular way and gives them the social status and liking they may seek.

If you want to be liked by others, you'll need to possess a certain amount of charisma and know how to best utilize and display it towards others. Your charisma can be a blessing towards and for you and it can also be a curse in some cases for displaying too much of it or doing it incorrectly can make you look like an idiot or a fool in front of others.

The art of using energy with charisma and persuasive techniques.

Your charisma is extremely unique to you, and it is the signature by which you actually speak to others through your energy, your own unique, interpersonal power and your own beautiful words there is a way in art of being able to use your social skills and put together those abilities along with your energetic abilities, and your charisma in order to produce a masterful means of being able to communicate with others and influence others using these specific techniques.

This technique you're mastering is the art of persuasion that you'll need to utilize to convince, influence and persuade others that you're a worthy amazing charismatic influential and cool person that they want to bring friends with or need to be around or that you're unique and great or fun.

Many people seek to be influential people towards others, and they want others to listen to what they have to say, and make sure that their words count and matter.

A positive perspective in life is what is needed to become an influential person to others along with using your charisma and energy in order to be able to get people to like or want to be around you.

What exactly is energy and what are energetic abilities? Everybody has their own energy that they use and that exist internally within them, but most people do not harness their energy or tap into it or attempt to use it for any means. People generate positive energy, but people are oblivious to their own energetic forces and abilities. If you'd like to be positive and influential, you'll need to know how to use your energy for different reasons and how to utilize it properly and specifically.

Entertaining charisma, energy, and your persuasive techniques

In order to completely master, the art of persuasion, you'll need to intertwine your energy, your charisma, and your abilities and persuasive techniques in order to be able to create an extremely gifted notion of mastering the art of persuasion and a fully charismatic amazing human being, who has developed their art and skill perfectly of being able to speak with others with politeness, charisma, energy, and entertainment. The enmeshment of these qualities can create a beautiful energetic scenario of a person being able to create a personality and exuberance that exudes energy and personalities towards others that can cause people to want to be around you or to like you.

Entertaining these different characteristics and putting them all together will allow you to skillfully be able to master the art of influence persuasion, but it will take some time in practice before it happens naturally and automatically for you, though for many people it does occur naturally and automatically, however, there are methods by which you can actually learn to utilize these techniques, gifts and abilities, and become an extremely charismatic individual who can easily influence manipulate others. And be an extremely likable personality towards others, and someone who people want to be around and who people love and who you might consider to be the life of the party and the center of attention

Your social skills and persuasive and influential techniques become a beautiful work of art that you used to interact and every day dealings with others is something that you recognize and are able to become better and better at.

When you attempt to persuade or influence others, it's important to use a few techniques and skills

Never force your opinions on others

It's imperative to not force your opinions or beliefs on others. Everyone is entitled to their beliefs and their mindset and way of thinking; however, you have learned the art of persuasion so like any salesperson you're well able to manipulate others into feeling or believing the concepts you feel or believe and know and can do so artistically using your newfound sales abilities and tactics. It's important to use your great social talents and skills to manipulate and persuade people into the feelings and thoughts you may want them to feel or believe in, under the pretense and limitations of good and not under the guise of anything extremely evil, selfish, or manipulative.

Display your beliefs and opinions with friendliness

It's imperative to exert extreme friendliness in order to gain what you want, for being sweet is what works, and anyone can get anything with honey and sugar, not with malice, greed, anger or hatred. If you're extremely friendly towards others, they'll generally tend to perceive you as a non-threat and will cease to hold any animosity towards you and will trust and like you more and enjoy your company far more than if you were negative or sour towards them, arrogant, callous, or boisterous.

When you approach anyone, you need to do so with the act of major friendliness and a friendly open-minded personable attitude for this is what will help you gain what you need with others- positivity, confidence and open-minded friendliness. Positivity is the most important tactic you can use when you speak to others in a social setting, and being the utmost positive person will allow you to be likeable, friendly and will want others to want to be your friend and want to be around your good energy.

Never display any form of coercion or a sales tactic approach

It's imperative to never use coercion or a sales tactic approach to anything that you do in life, and that you focus on being persuasive without coercive or forcing others into feeling or believing your opinions, feelings, thoughts and beliefs. If you do use coercion, it generally will not work because negative tactics do not allow for people to want to have any part of you or be your friend. This is not a way to win someone over.

If you want to win someone over, you need to use extreme amounts of kindness, good, humbleness, wisdom, good energy, articulacy, intellect, charisma, and any other positive beneficial characteristic you can think of. Once you're able to master using the art of positivity and charisma to gain the influence of others, you'll be able to win people over and be a success in anything you do, especially the area of social interaction.

Use your energy and charisma in social interactions

How to influence others

In order to be able to influence others, you will need to use your charisma and all the energy and passion that you possess within yourself and skillfully master the technique of being able to show off this charisma energetically. Most people wouldn't understand this particular concept because they do not understand how energy works and functions and do not tend to think about energy or energetic interactions. However, energetic interactions exist in our everyday life and people speak and do tasks jobs and deeds using their energy and use it to influence them and others. A good example of this would be using your energetic abilities to enhance our sales abilities. If you are a sales person, many people who work in function and sales actually use their energies to be of extreme positivity towards others, and they use their energy to actually influence other people and get them to purchase or buy things from them.

Energetic interactions exist in our everyday life and to be or a great influence to others you'll need to learn how to tap into your own personal power and energies and practice using and developing it and know how to control it and use it to attract, affect and have a type of influence on others. What this means is you'll have to learn how to give your energy to others or manipulate others using it however this can only be done in a non-intrusive position means that is there solely to benefit a person and influence them in a positive manner not a negative one.

You might say, what exactly does this mean and how on earth can I utilize the energy that I do possess and how do I tap into it? I've never heard of anything like this before. If you haven't heard of energy, then you might be like a large number of people, though most people understand their own energies on some level and know how to utilize their energy in order to be able to affect our influence others especially those and sales positions or any day every day positions in life and those who have to deal or interact with people on a regular basis.

Energy is one of the key factors and influence when it comes to dealing with and interacting with people on a regular basis and one of the few ingredients you'll need to become a master at the art of persuasion and manipulation. The art of persuasion and manipulation should never be done on a negative basis to influence or use your abilities for negative gain, which should only be used in an extremely positive manner for once a person begins committing, treacherous acts of negativity it becomes an effect on them that will continue to occur and that they will continue to do without care or any form of morality or guilt.

While energetic interactions are the key to being able to manipulate and influence others, through direct energetic means or even manipulation, there are other key factors which allow a person to be able to influence others. This is the energy coupled with social charisma which allows for the interactions to take place on a smooth basis and allows a person to use their energies to be able to manipulate people as they want or need, as well as utilizing their social and speaking skills to do this.

This can involve speaking to others with extreme articulation, intelligence, charisma, and great amounts of energy present. A person will want to practice putting together all of these elements in order to create a gracious and harmonious vibe to use in order to effectively communicate with others using their newfound techniques and gifts. Once you've become a master at communicating effectively using these abilities, it becomes easier for you to do so in various social settings and with different people.

The Art Of Manipulation

The art of manipulation is a tool used by some in order to gain ground and higher ground over others in in order to exert a specific level of superiority and social dominance over others. This is an egregious act that should never be done or taken into consideration for manipulating others for social gains, or your own selfish benefits is only going to harm to everybody in the long run. The more negativity and evil you commit in this world, the more negative karma is accrued unto you in this life and many other lives and worlds. It is of extreme importance that you do not accrue anymore negative karma and create the snowballing effect of committing evil because once you commit evil, it comes back at you and forces you to do more and more of it. There are many people who harness positive energy to do negative deeds and actions and this is something that is frowned upon, and that should not be done in any way shape or form.

It needs to be taken into effect when it comes to a person who is committing these treacherous acts against themselves and against others whereby they are creating disharmony in the universe, and in the planet, and these actions should not be utilized, except in a positive and beneficial manner towards a person and those around them.

Chapter 3

How To Gain Friends and Win People Over

Do you make friends easily or is it a challenge in your life to be able to make friends and do things that are of influence and significance? Do you have goals that you've set for yourself in your life? You will have to ask yourself these questions in order to get a better understanding of who you are as a person and what you represent. There are ways to get people to like you and to win friends over and to influence people. However, the key goal is for you to like and love yourself first, for once you do, only then will you be able to get others to want to be around you and want to be your friend or believe you are an exceptional person. Do you possess natural charisma or is this something you will need to work on? You should set goals in your life to assist you with attempting to be able to gain better friendships, relationships and win people over. Is there a man or woman in your life who you are enthralled with or who you want to like you in some format?

How to get people to want a relationship with you

Relationships can be difficult and challenging circumstances. Life is full of ups and downs and it's not always easy to find someone in a person's life. People go through all kinds of challenges when it comes to getting to be with someone, dating, life, and many other aspects of this world. Is there someone in particular who you like, yet you're not sure if they'll want to be with you back, or maybe you've tried being with them yet they haven't shown much interest? This can always be a very unfortunate situation. It's definitely not fun when you seek the attention and desire of someone and they aren't interested in you back. They have decided they simply don't care for you, or maybe they feel you're not good enough for them. They may not feel a spark between the two of you either, or you're just not their type.

Take no heed- there are ways to get someone to want to be with you and to make yourself far more attractive to them than they think you are or to make yourself seem better and more appealing to them in general.

You'll want to exude confidence and charisma and use the mastered art of persuasion that you've learned, gained and discovered to be able to show them that you're an amazing individual who is full of love, life, personality, energy and charisma. You'll want to display to them that you're an extrovert who is likeable and friendly, if that is their type of course. Some people may not want to be around an extrovert and may actually want to deal with or be around more of an introverted person. if that is the case, then you'll want to mold yourself in that kind of person and be the type of person that they truly want to be with.

1. Express your desire for them
2. Show them you care about them immensely
3. Believe in them and give them unlimited moral support
4. Show them you're an amazing person to be with
5. Believe in yourself and exude extreme amounts of confidence
6. Build immense chemistry between the two of you
7. Make yourself seem more appealing to them
8. Mold yourself into being who they want to be with

Ways to gain friends and make people like you

Be a naturally friendly person

To be a naturally friendly person is the easiest, most rational and simplest form of displaying personable communication skills and being likeable towards others and causing others to like you, enjoy your company or want to be around you. Many people out there have a natural knack for being very friendly, while others seem bitter, angry or unfriendly. If you want to make a lot of friends in this world and in life, you will want to be extremely friendly and polite to people for it will show them you're an open-minded, nice, kind individual who they may want to incorporate into their circle of friends, you're easy to please and eager to please others, and that you're laid-back, down to earth and humble.

Be charismatic and likable

Be charismatic in your everyday social interactions and very likable! Many people are of course but it's important to present your social charisma to others, along with your beautiful energy and to be very likable to people, for people respond very well to those with good energy, happiness, and good charisma. Charisma is an exceptional and beautiful trait to have and you'll want to exude confidence, good energy, positivity, a great personality, and amazing charisma towards others and in social settings.

Show people that you're not shy, boastful, arrogant, or someone with negative connotations or ideations about them. Display to people what they want to perceive and see in a person which is someone who is full of love, life, energy, beauty, charisma, and many other personable fun-loving traits.

Stay away from being negative and pessimistic

People often enjoy the company of very positive, friendly, kind, energetic people. People tend to love extroverts and will want to be around them most of the time. They really do not care for pessimistic or negative people and don't want to be around negativity or people complaining about themselves or aspects in their life. It's important to always be positive and kind and stray from being negative or pessimistic in general. Once you do this, you'll find yourself loving life more and find yourself with more people surrounding you who want to be around you, rather than get away from you.

Act like you're the life of the party

Extroverts tend to be liked most of the time and people want to be around those who are the life of the party, energetic, outgoing, bubbly and who have a great and exuberant personality. If you're in a social setting, you'll want to speak loudly, boldly and with confidence, be fun personable and likeable and act like you are the life of the party most of the time. Practice putting on a show with friends and family and displaying this wonderful and special personality, attitude and part of yourself to the general people that you socialize and interact with. This will often help you get more friends or people to be around you.

Exude nothing but confidence and exuberance

Exuding confidence and care and a great personality will help you go far if you're trying to get people to like you. Act suave, dress nice and present yourself with confidence and people will generally flock to you or want to be around you. Acting shy, pessimistic, closed-off, fearful or frightened will deter people from wanting to be around you. Be sure in your dealings with people, display signs of being increasingly on top of your game and above others and you'll get people to want to figure out your allure and want to be around you all the time.

Dress very nice all the time and show others that you're a suave and personable confident, neat, clean person who dresses nice and who others would want to be around. Display all the great qualities of a successful person and you'll attract the attention of whoever you want.

Display a great and wonderful personality

Displaying a vibrant and wonderful personality can aid and assist with getting people to want to be near you or around you and with gaining friends and winning people over. You'll need to showcase who you are and your personality to others and also know what type you are and what kind of person you are.

Be honest and open with others

Be honest and open with others. Display a good amount of honesty and kindness. Show people you're good and that you're not a fake or a liar. People don't want to be around those who are two-faced, backstabbers, or anyone with any negative or downplaying qualities. They want to be around those who are confident, interesting, funny, likable, nice, kind, good, generous, decent and honest people. Be yourself first and foremost and be as honest as you can about yourself, your love and who you are. Trying to hide parts of yourself or who you are with the attempts of trying to make friends doesn't always work. Of course, you don't want to go around telling everyone about the skeletons in your closet either, but you will want to be an upfront, open, genuine person because people love the company of genuine, good people.

Speak with energy, drive, and enthusiasm

Speak with energy, drive, confidence, and great enthusiasm. It is imperative that you speak with drive and passion and not just as someone who doesn't care, mumbles, or lacks passion, drive or care for most aspects in the world or in life. Speak with great confidence, be loud and bold if you can be and be very confident in your dealings with others. Articulate your words and speech, and don't come across as shy or someone who is unsure of themselves. This will attract more people to you in the long run.

Chapter 4

How To Have Social Confidence

People may feel as if it's a good idea to please themselves. They live in a world full of ideations of shallowness and selfishness sometimes. However, rather than living in a reality full of seeking to please ourselves, we should be wanting to please and help others in many different forms. We should be living in a world full of selflessness, and a place where we're attempting to make friends for the greater good of our own lives and for the lives of those close to us as well.

Living for the sake of good

We should exist and live for the sake of goodness, honesty and truth. While people may want to use their abilities, confidence and social skills to better themselves, it should be done for the good of others. Goodness is a part of our everyday world and reality. We don't fully comprehend or understand the concept of living under the golden rule in our lives through we need to. When we please others, we shouldn't be doing it so we can win others over or influence people, but for the greater good of others and of humanity.

Social Confidence

Social confidence is a very integral part of being on this planet and you'll want to possess confidence in your social life in order to build the foundations for being a charismatic person and being of influence to others. How can a person have social confidence in their life and world? What exactly is the concept of having confidence in social settings or interactions?

Well, the truth is, most people just simply don't think about the social interactions they do have or examine the methods by which they communicate with others or have learned the art of introspection or fully understand how it all works. Many people simply socially interact with one another or are too scared to interact and may have varying forms of social phobias such as social anxiety or social fear. We live in a world where people are often judged for being too shy, too anxious, or not confident enough in a social setting. Often, if we don't show others that we exude a certain amount of confidence, they will form their own opinions of who we are or call people shy or form other derogatory opinions about them.

One thing you'll want to stray away from is being called 'shy.' Often, people in social settings will nitpick and choose specific people to label as 'shy.' Sometimes, it's even a form of social dominance in order to put someone down and act as if a person is above another person. In order to never be called or labeled 'shy', you will always want to exude a certain level of social confidence, charisma, boldness, and assertiveness.

How to be assertive socially

Being assertive is an important aspect of displaying social confidence, as is being bold in your interactions with others. You'll rarely want to be 'quiet' in an interaction, though many times, there are people who are introverts who generally will sit back and allow others to talk. Sometimes, you're just allowing others to talk or give their opinion when the label of 'shy' may be thrown at you. In order to be more assertive, you'll want to talk louder than others and speak in more bold, confident, assertive tone, rather than speaking softly or nicely. Many times, people who are kind nice, or even introverts, tend to speak softly or in a very nice or polite manner, and though that is the correct way to speak to others, it may not always help you in social interactions.

Are you an introvert or an extrovert?

Are you an introvert or an extrovert? It's important to figure this out and ask yourself this important question, for whether you're an introvert or extrovert will greatly affect the manner in which you perceive a social situation and how you interact with others. Introverts tend to be very closed in social situations and tend to be excellent and good listeners and will often sit back and allow others to do the talking. They may talk softly or low in tone and may be perceived as shy or having some form of social anxiety or awkwardness.

Introverts tend to focus on experiences that are internal rather than external. They prefer to be alone and enjoy time alone, or with a small group of people. They are often self-aware and reflective people. They tend to be very good listeners and establish trust with others through good listening habits. They also prefer to have one-on-one interactions, rather than large group interactions. If you're an introvert, you'll need to learn to come out of your shell and be more similar to an extrovert, if you want to be able to win people over and make more friends in your life.

Extroverts perceive social interactions very differently from introverts. They tend to be very open-minded, talk loudly and boldly, are the life of the party and often are loud and boisterous. Extroverts are extremely sociable, and they have many different friends and enjoy being around large groups of people. They are very talkative, energetic and feel energized by being around others and in social settings. They are often optimistic and enjoy taking risks in many cases.

Extroverts are often the life of the party and can easily win friends over, influence others, and though they may not have discovered or mastered the art of persuasion or influence, they still have extreme amounts of social confidence, and are confident in the actions they do undergo or pursue, as opposed to the introvert who might live along the lines of fear-based thinking and ideas sometimes.

Having social confidence can take great skills and expertise. Sometimes it takes a lot of charisma and other aspects of a person to be able to display this part of themselves. For some people it just doesn't exist, yet for others it is very vivacious and is something that can be displayed very easily.

Social anxiety

There are people out there who possess social anxiety. They have an intense fear of social interactions and dealings with people in general. Social anxiety is a dangerous and painful stigma for someone to have to deal with or endure. People often live in a fear-based world where they fear what people may think of them, are scared of how they come across socially and are in dire need of assistance when it comes to developing their social confidence.

This is a psychological situation or condition which is displayed by intense fear or anxiety in social situations often due to concerns about being embarrassed, judged or rejected. It can lead to avoidance of social interactions and significantly impact a person's life. People fear being judged or rejected by others. They avoid social situations that cause distress or fear, and they experience intense anxiety and fear in social situations. They are often unable to effectively socially interact with others. Those with social anxiety are in dire need of therapy and mental health and need practice interacting with others and getting over the fears they have. They are in dire need of help from others when it comes to developing social confidence, for they are in the spectrum or class of people who simply do not possess any social confidence whatsoever. Therapy and medication, along with CBT can greatly help those with social anxiety. Those with social anxiety, however, can still develop social confidence and will need to in order to be able to learn how to develop the art of making friends, being charismatic in social settings and winning people over.

Chapter 5

Your Friends Are A Goldmine For You

Your friends are there to help and benefit you but not in a selfish aggrandizing or narcissistic way. They are in fact there to be beacons of good and light for you and to help you achieve your goals, to be companions to you, to be friends and confidantes to you and to be your supporters in a time of need. Your perspective towards the concept of who your friends are needs to change. Many people have a flawed perception and feel as if people are there solely for their benefit or there to please them in some form. People use people as they want and even use and abuse them.

The purpose of having friends: there is a hidden purpose to having friends. Who are your friends? Do you have a large number of people in your life who you can call your friends who can support you and who you can support, love, bless and be a part of? Your great purpose for having friends in your life should be to benefit you and them in a harmonious positive mutual way and to enjoy each other's company and each other's lives. Friends are a blessing to us in many forms, though sometimes people take them for granted or have friends for other reasons which may seem selfish in nature. People may feel as if they need their friends or a friend for companionship or for company or for other reasons.

Why do you have friends, and have you ever examined the notion of why you do have people in your life who you care about and are around for long periods of time? Do you need someone to confide in? Someone to hang out with? Do you do this for mutual reasons or for your own self-serving reasons? Do you seek to have more friends for the sole benefit of numbers or to stroke your ego?

Your friends should be a gold mine for you. They are sentient creations there to benefit and support you and in turn you are there to help and support them as well. This mutual harmony is a gifted blessing for the each of you and assists you in your life and world while being companions to each other as well. And yes! Having friends is a fun, great, amazing special experience to love internally, be happy about and to share with others. Most people are proud of their friends and may even gloat about them to others. They feel as if their friends are special and the bond, they hold with each other is very special.

People sometimes feel as if friends are there solely to benefit them or to do things for them, but this is not the case in many given situations. Friends are often there for mutual benefit or for each person to do good things for each other and to be of assistance to one another. There are many factors that a friendship possesses that can be of benefit to a person and can help a person become better overall and gain and grow from the situation.

Do you cherish your friends, or do you take them for granted? Many people do cherish their friends, while others take them for granted and act as if their friends are there to help them or just feel as if they've always been there for them if that is the case. Your friends may be helpful to you in a time of need and may always be there for you, which is a great thing, though sometimes there may be issues or rifts that have been there or may occur or exist as a result of intermingling and other issues.

Your friends are truly a goldmine for you and can be there not only to assist and support you, but also to help you build and grow as a person and create and establish connections with other people as well. They can help you in many various areas in your life not only in one or two different ones. They can help you in dealing with various situations in your life and world and can assist you with becoming a better person and growing in your life and world and with elevating yourself as a person.

It's important to be there for your friends as well in their times of need and to always put your friends' needs above yours. Your needs are very important too, but those close to you matter the most and it's good to make sure they are incredibly happy and doing well and not in any situation where they are made to feel down, inferior, or upset.

Friendships can be a huge benefit for others and can have many positive amazing last effects for people in general. Some of these benefits include:

Mental support

Friends provide unlimited mental support and can aid in giving a person different kinds of support and other mental health benefits. If someone is down, they can always look to a friend for fun and mutual support and aiding them in their world and life. If you have any issues going on in your life or are in need of advice or comfort, a friend can be there to assist you in many different ways.

Boost happiness

Friendship tends to be about sacrificing our happiness for our friend's happiness, and we tend to want our friends to be incredibly happy, so many people in healthy, loving and good friendships will find themselves very happy as people are putting other's needs above theirs when it comes to happiness. Having a loving, healthy friendship will often boost your happiness levels and keep you a very healthy and happy person.

Overcome stress

Friendships tend to help a person overcome stress in various forms. Stress-related activities can become a part of someone's normal life and people tend to focus on these aspects. People need to focus on being healthy and happy people and having healthy, positive friendships can assist a person with overcoming any form of stress or any major issues in their life. It is a very positive and beneficial thing for someone.

Personal growth

Friendships help a person build personal growth. They aid and assist a person in building themselves up and being better people in general. Friendships can create many diverse situations in a person's life and can really help someone build lots of growth in their personal lives and professional lives as well. Being of assistance to others and doing nice things for them can really help with a person's mental and personal growth.

Friendships challenge us to grow and evolve. Friends often act as mirrors, reflecting our strengths and weaknesses. They provide very helpful feedback and encourage us to step out of our comfort zones. Through friendships, we learn valuable life skills such as empathy, communication, and conflict resolution. Friends inspire us to become better versions of ourselves and support us in our personal journeys.

Reduce loneliness

Friendships definitely help reduce loneliness in someone's life. They allow a person to expand their social circle and build sustainable wonderful relationships with really great, friendly and amazing people and allow a person to not be lonely in their life in general.

Friends provide company and alleviate feelings of loneliness. They help with dealing with situations in life and can help during times of need or crisis. You never have to be alone if you have friends in your world.

Improve your mental health

Friendships improve mental health significantly. Without friends or a friendship, a person might struggle mentally and socially and be alone without any real support, yet with friends in someone's life, they are doing great, and their mental health is supported and helped by their friendships. They can go out and do things with people, go to places, and find ways and reasons to enjoy their life. Having a cherished important friendship can do wonders for a person and is a very important part of being in this world.

A sense of belonging

Friendships allow a person to feel a sense of belonging in a huge way. Friends help you cultivate a sense of community and allow you to feel as if you belong to a group of people whether it's a small circle of friends or a larger group such as a church, youth group, or other group type setting. When you go out and find people you know, you'll feel much better about yourself and feel a strong sense of belonging and as if you're part of a greater community. This is an integral part of existing on this planet and being in this world.

How to win more friends in life

Winning friends in life may not always be easy or simple. For some people it seems really easy. Do you have a friend or family member who just always seems to have tons of friends and people just flock to them for some reason and the same just doesn't seem to happen for you? For some people, making friends is extremely easy and it just seems to happen for them, yet for others it does take a lot more effort and time and even practice.

For some people, it takes practice to be able to make friends and win and gain people's confidence, liking, love or approval. It takes practice, repetition, great social skills, being likeable, having confidence and loving yourself in order to be able to get people to like you or want to be around you. Not everyone has great social skills, and some people have different forms of social anxiety and find it much harder to talk to people and have a harder time being social in general.

Cultivating friendships is an extremely important part of being on this planet and we need friends in order to grow and live in this world. Without friendships, a person finds themselves alone, without help, support or comfort and may have a difficult time in life or during times of crisis. With friends around, everything becomes easier for a person, they can gain better self-esteem, enjoy their life more, feel a sense of company and togetherness and their life becomes better.

Your friends are a goldmine for you whether you know it or not. They are there to help and support you and be your amazing great confidantes. They are there to be of assistance to you during any times of need or when you feel you are down or in any form of despair. You will have a much better and fulfilled life if you tend to generate healthy friendships and if you have a healthy social circle with a large number of people there to support, aid, and benefit you.

Chapter 6

Using Your Talents And Abilities

Your talents and abilities are a part of you, yet you may not know about how they work and how you can utilize them. You possess many God-given talents that you may not know of and it's important to be able to know what they are and how to use them in your everyday life, and in your social dealings and interactions. Your talents should be used to the best of your abilities and also in social interactions since you can use them to help and benefit you in many ways. What are your talents and abilities? How do you plan on using them to benefit you in your everyday and social interactions? Are you talented in any given areas in life?

You'll want to examine what areas in life you're talented in and how you'd like to use those abilities to better your life and career and what kind of person and story you'd like to present to others when it comes to your abilities and all the different facets involved.

Improving your social skills

Social skills are an integral part of our everyday world. Social interactions take place on a daily basis, but most people don't' fully comprehend why they act or behave the way they do. It is good to know exactly why you do behave or act the way you do so you can progress when it comes to your social interactions. Your interactions with people are important in your world, though you may not have hurdled or understood how to be the charismatic person that others are.

In order to be able to do well in many areas of life, such as business, relationships, work, and friendships, you'll want to be able to develop many aspects of your social skills and make sure that you know how to effectively and successfully interact with others on a daily basis that benefits your life.

1. Display empathy: It's important to display enormous amounts of empathy towards others- for showing others that you have empathy and caring about them will allow you to benefit and gain more friendships and showing that

you care will in turn cause others to give back to you what you're showing towards them. Displaying empathy in general for a given situation causes people to want to embrace your presence and you and will allow you to further develop your social abilities.

2. Create goals for yourself: Create goals to become a better person socially and set these goals and begin practicing how to speak to people and how to better talk to others effectively and how to promote active listening and be a better person and friend.

3. Improve your listening skills: People enjoy, and love being heard and acknowledged. It's important to improving your listening abilities towards others and in everyday life, conversations, work, and in most activities that you participate in. This will allow you to improve your social skills because you'll receive more positive feedback from those around you.

4. Master the art of small talk: Small talk can be crucial for building relationships with people. It's good to learn the basics of communicating with people and trying to build rapport and learning more about someone or being able to communicate ideas effectively this way.

5. Engage with others: Engaging with others can assist a person into becoming a better social communicator. You can practice with family and friends as far as talking to people and social skills are concerned.

6. Talk about positive things: Talking about positive things can be a great benefit to others and speaking in negative tones is something that can be a negative benefit to people. It's important to speak in a positive manner and not allow others to perceive you as negative or see the negative in things or conversations you're having. This will create a better environment between the people you're interacting with and make you a better communicator.
7. Improve your body language: Social skills aren't always about verbal communication. There are many non-verbal cues involved and it's imperative that you use these non-verbal cues to interact with others and better communicate with people. You can use hand gestures, signs, facial gestures to enhance your social skills and communication abilities.
8. Be someone who compliments others: It's a good idea to compliment others, for people enjoy being praised or brought up and it helps or allows people to further appreciate your good nature and positive remarks and will in turn cause people to compliment you as well and creates a very positive social environment.
9. Display extroversion: Be extroverted in a conversation. Be bold, assertive and even show that you care about a person or their situation. exude confidence and energy and learn to speak out loud in a group setting. This will allow you to build on your social abilities and skills.

Your talents and abilities are a huge part of your make-up. If you want to persuade and influence others, you will want to utilize your great given talents and abilities in any way you can in order to be able to pursue the art of confidence and social interaction and persuasion.

Your persuasive skills and talents that you've learned to develop and that which you've honed can be used in a very beneficial manner in order to further develop your social skills and learn how to influence and gain more people in your life who call themselves your friends. You will also want to use your own natural abilities that include your own social skills, friendliness, gifts of persuasion and influence that you may possess within in order to better yourself in your given situation.

Chapter 7

HOW TO LOVE YOURSELF FIRST

Loving yourself first is one of the key methods and ways for getting people to enjoy your company and like you. For you cannot engage in the love of others without loving yourself first. In order to be able to influence others in a positive and beneficial way, you'll want to love yourself first and foremost.

You are the key person in your world and matter the most to yourself and even to others. You're not a worthless or unimportant individual, you matter in this world and amongst others too. Your thoughts, feelings and beliefs matter more than anything and you should focus on self-love in order to be able to help others. For without loving yourself, you're unable to handle loving others and do not have the capacity to love others in different forms.

Do you care about yourself? Do you ever practice self-care and take the time out to give yourself any ample time to heal from past issues or love yourself currently for any issues you're having to go through. It's imperative to care for yourself and worry about committing to self-care techniques, in order to become a better person for yourself and for those who are close to you such as family and friends.

There are many different means and methods of practicing self-care from going to the spa to relax or getting an amazing massage. It includes healthy eating, mindfulness, meditative techniques, and emotional support through journaling or talking to friends, and even setting boundaries.

Loving yourself is a beautiful gift and facet that not everyone has the capability of doing. Many people don't possess the notion of love within them and don't really care to feel love towards themselves or take their own selves for granted in some form. It's of grave importance to have feelings for the things that you do and love you for doing the things you do in life. Do you do anything special that you're proud of? Are you good or talented at a specific thing? It's of sheer importance that you are proud of the accomplishments you've achieved and that you focus on being a kind person to yourself and constantly show yourself goodness and kindness. You are a gracious and wonderful person inside who loves to be around others and be jubilant in your adventures and in life.

It's of utmost importance that you live your life through the lens of love and goodness, and that you're constantly bringing yourself up and doing what you can to harness good energy towards yourself, for this will allow you to gain and build the confidence you desire and allow you to become a more confident person on all levels. You are a wonderful special person, and you will need to know and believe this in order to be able to understand your abilities, talents and who you are deep inside. Influence comes from within- from your own life and using your abilities to change the way people think and changing their lives.

In order to love yourself, you will need to practice self-compassion by being kind to yourself, forgiving past mistakes, celebrating your accomplishments, setting healthy boundaries, prioritizing self-care, and embracing your unique qualities, all while actively working to cultivate positive self-talk and gratitude for who you are.

Some important aspects of self-love include:

- ♥ **Positive self-talk:** Replace negative thoughts with affirming statements about yourself. Nurture regular positive self-talk and affirmations and statements that are there to enhance your confidence and other good aspects within you.

- ♥ **Self-forgiveness:** Accept that everyone makes mistakes and learn to let go of past regrets. Forgive yourself for anything you feel you have done that you may not approve of or that you feel you regret. Accept the mistakes you've made and love yourself for the good actions you take.
- ♥ **Self-care routine:** Prioritize activities that nourish your physical and mental well-being, like healthy eating, exercise, and relaxation techniques. Have a regular self-care routine that you have established that will allow you to excel in your world and develop healthy and beneficial habits for yourself.
- ♥ **Set boundaries:** Learn to say no and prioritize your needs to protect your energy. Learn to recognize negative patterns and behaviors and not allow them into your world in any way. Setting boundaries allows for a person to further develop more self-love and compassion not only for themselves, but for others as well.
- ♥ **Practice gratitude:** Focus on the positive aspects of your life and appreciate your strengths. Always be grateful for any given aspect in your life and never take for granted the beautiful wonders that are present in your world.
- ♥ **Embrace your uniqueness:** Celebrate what makes you different and special. You are a unique special and amazing person and it's important that you embrace these very aspects of yourself, rather than feel as if you're not anyone important or special or as if perceiving your differences is

something that is negative when it's something positive and great.

- ♥ **Be patient in general:** Understand that self-love is a journey and allow yourself to make mistakes while learning and growing.
- ♥ **Know yourself well:** It is imperative that you know yourself very well. In order to be able to practice self-love, you will want to have a higher understanding of your own intentions and actions or a higher awareness of these things. You will want to know yourself and how you feel towards any given aspect of your actions or intent in life. This will allow you to develop a greater sense of self-love and allow your confidence to become greater, your self-compassion and for these aspects in your life to skyrocket.

Self-love consists of a wondrous, patient and beautiful method to loving and giving to yourself with every part of your very being. It allows you to delve deep into yourself and focus on the core being that you are the part of yourself that possesses unlimited capabilities and love and allows you to be greater than you ever thought you could be.

It is critical to our overall well-being and studies show that we do need self-love in order to take action, changes, and move onto new opportunities. Self-love motivates most of our positive behavior and reduces harmful behavior. It helps us take care of ourselves, lower stress and aim for success in every aspect of our world. It also empowers us to take risks and say no to things that aren't beneficial for us.

Benefits of Self-Love

Lowers Stress

Self-love tends to lower stress levels in a person's body, mind, spirit, and life and allows for greater resilience in their world when it comes to anything that is happening. If you have a sense of self-love and if it is strong, then you're greater able to tackle any challenges or issues you're dealing with in life.

Self-love is directly linked to aspects of self-compassion. Together, they work hand in hand and allow a person to become more resilient and able to deal with challenges in life and become overall happier people.

Builds Confidence

The more self-love you possess, the more you can handle influencing others because you better believe in yourself, your ideals and beliefs and in the aspects that exist in your life. You will have a strong sense of belief in yourself and your ideals in general and will have a better concept of how to help and deal with other people. Your mental acuity will also become enhanced in many ways.

Allows You To Grow

Having self-love for oneself allows a person to grow not only in confidence, but also as a person and in general. When you love yourself, you're able to identify both opportunities for growth and chances for you to shine. This allows a person to take chances in their life and to help growth in their world and build themselves up to take on new chapters in their life and to accomplish tasks and goals they may not have done so yet.

Growth in Empathy

Self-love allows a person to grow in empathy and become more kind, giving, caring and empathetic people in general. When we are able to see ourselves and understand and accept our weaknesses and strengths with compassion and sympathy, we can also learn to have enormous amounts of compassion for others. This ability to hold space for other people's issues and situations helps us to become more empathetic. In turn, empathy creates a stronger connection with us and with others as well.

Set Boundaries

Loving oneself regularly allows a person to be able to develop great amounts of self-compassion, love, confidence, and personal understanding and can let a person establish healthy and good boundaries for a person. It's important to establish boundaries for a person's own self in order to not allow toxic or negative behavior to become inserted into a person's general life and world. When a person learns how to establish boundaries and not allow any form of negativity into their life, it has a snowball effect that lets positive behaviors and self-love to grow within a person along with confidence, happiness, and good.

Chapter 8

BEING OF INFLUENCE TO OTHERS IN A POSITIVE WAY

Being of influence to others in a positive way should be one of a person's main goals in life. To be able to influence others is a wonderful quality that a person can have and is something that is not easily accomplished. Not everyone can be of an inspiration to others, yet there are people who truly seek to want this and others who really don't care to be in this kind of situation.

Are you an inspirational person?

Have you ever thought of yourself as an inspirational person? Do you possess talents and gifts that inspire others? Do you possess the gift of gab or influence naturally? If you answered yes to any of these questions, then you're doing extremely good for yourself! People who inspire others aren't always easy to come by and there are many people out there looking for role models, heroes and inspirations in order to better influence their own lives.

Many out there seek to inspire others, while others don't have the knack in them to want to inspire people or assist others with becoming better people, growing in their gifts or talents, or allowing them to be able to see who they truly are deep within.

Do you have what it takes to inspire others or are you someone who doesn't believe or feel in being of great influence to others and being an inspiration? There are celebrities out there today and people all over the internet who seek to be an inspiration to others. Because of social media, this concept has grown and increased in significance, and there are masses out there who enjoy being a role model and figure to others to look up to and who people want to be like or who are able to showcase their gifts or talents to others.

Being of influence and inspiration to others is a great gift that a person should be proud of and something that many people don't generally think of or are aware of. If you seek to influence others in a positive way, it's usually an internal feeling you've had for a long time and a mission of yours or anyone who feels this way. It's a wonderful mission to be on in general and you'll want to embrace it any way you can, rather than ignore or question it.

According to the dictionary, the word influence is the power to change or affect someone or something. Many people can cause changes without directly forcing it to happen. There is no limitation to who or what you can influence, and it can be used in life in any form.

The ability to influence somebody or something to change without using force is a strong sign of an effective leader. Think of those times when a little bit of influence might have swung things in your favor. Those pivotal moments were not failures but missed opportunities. You knew you could have done something but didn't know what to do.

The art of being an influential person comes from wanting to be of a great influence to others and to the masses and is something that many people do on a general basis though those who are most acknowledged for it tend to be famous people such as athletes, actors, actresses, singers and other famous people of influence. People in everyday life are of great influence to others including teachers, lawyers, doctors, professors, sales people or anyone in any profession literally.

You'll seek to want to inspire others in a positive way or change the way people think but generally in a very positive inspirational manner. Famous people are of great influence to others and inspire people to become better people, athletes, talents, singers, writers, doctors, actors and allow people to be better in many aspects they do in their life or world.

Inspiration comes from within

Inspiration generally starts from within. People generally don't always seek to be leaders of their world but when they have the ability to do or the internal inspiration then they will. A person has the ability to influence others in a positive way, change their life, teach other people about their own personal power which in turn will allow them to become better people, more effective leaders and do a great number of things in this world to better it. As humans, this should be our goal and dream- to better this planet and to inspire others to change tehri ways of thinking and to better themselves so they can be of benefit and influence to others as well. It becomes a great snowball effect, and this is what the concept of influence truly is.

Once a person changes their life, their perspective and their world, they will far more easily be able to inspire and influence others into becoming better people because they will be living the morals and values of the way of goodness and greatness and will allow others to live and be this way as well. Living a life of wellness, good, and practicing the art of self-care will allow you to harness vast amounts of positive and good energies that you can utilize in your everyday life.

Being a leader in this world can occur in many different areas and arenas and in everyday life in general. Many people don't always seek to be leaders in their current position in life. Far too many people don't feel they are good enough to be leaders in their fields or even seek to be on top teaching or helping others. They'd rather stay as a sales agent, rather than being in a managerial position, or as a rental car agent over being a supervisor. Being a leader can put you in a place of great and effective influence over others and will teach you unlimited amounts of leadership abilities and allow you to become the leader and influential person you were meant to be or one that you have hoped and dreamed of.

You too can be of a great influence in this world and life, and you can do so by joining different areas in life and by focusing on being a better person in general, harnessing your internal positivity and happiness, spreading good to others, changing your perspective about life and the world in general and teaching and helping others what you have learned and put into practice.

There are several traits of goal-oriented leaders, and these traits display the type of leadership abilities and internal traits these people possess and what it takes to become a very influential person and leader in the world.

1. Goal-Oriented: Influential people are goal-oriented, and they exist by their very personal and business goals which they use to assist them with becoming more successful people. People are not typically influenced by people who do not have the concept of passion and integrity within them or those who just aren't successful in general.

2. Full of Integrity: Integrity is one of the most important assets a person should have if they seek to be a person of influence. It is the most essential aspect for success in personal development and personal growth. Integrity is probably the most essential quality for success in both professional development and personal growth. Integrity is valued by others because they want to trust and believe in a person who they're gaining benefit and lessons from so they seek to learn from a person who values honesty, goodness and integrity. It is the most essential element within the concept of personal influence and allows people to really look up to a person because that person is displaying ethics, morality and goodness rather than something negative or non-beneficial. In order to be of influence or benefit, you'll want to be beneficial, ethical, moral and upright and uphold impeccable morals and show this to others.

3. Optimistic: Researchers found in a study that a common quality of successful and influential people was a lot of optimism. Having a wonderful attitude is key to being a positive role model to others, and it is imperative you know how to display yourself around others along with a positive, influential and fun attitude to showcase your personality and who you are.

4. Sincere: Being sincere is very important when it comes to becoming a successfully influential person. This is because influential people generally tell the truth and are polite and kind and often sincere. Sincere people are generally warm and display trust to others.

The definition of sincere is free from pretense or deceit and proceeding from genuine feelings. Those who are genuinely good people are sincere and tend to do well when it comes to being of influence to others and that is because people are influenced by those who are good, sincere, and genuine and rarely want to be like people who are negative or bad.

5. Well-Informed and intelligent: Influential people are often well-informed about situations and possess extreme amounts of intellect and aren't stupid people. People look up to those who display intellect and who are well-informed about current situations in their life and in the world and who can rationalize situations and scenarios.

7. Loves People: Many people who are of good influence to others do love others and display patience, kindness, humility and other traits to show that they care about others. People love to be around others who actually care about them and who possess these traits. If you want to influence others in a positive way and in a greater manner, you will want to have these traits and practice having these traits when it comes to caring about others and loving and caring for them.

8. Communicates Effectively: It's important to be a very effective communicator in order to be of good influence to others.

Those who communicate well do excellent at helping others and people really look up to those who have great communication skills and who know how to talk to people.

9. Well-Mannered: Being well-mannered can really help a person do well in life and become successful. Well-mannered people are welcomed by others in huge ways and people love and enjoy being around them and treated well by them. Having good manners shows that you can treat others with respect, kindness, goodness and can be a better person in general.

10. Displays Perseverance: In the face of difficulty, perseverance and persistence are major qualities for success. Someone who is perseverant just shows that they can move forward with determination during hard times or times of adversity. Those who are generally of influence to others are very perseverant, good, decent people who during hard times show dedication, determination and caring attitudes.

Being an influential person requires persistence, motivation, dedication and many other facets in life. You can't just go from being someone who doesn't hold these qualities to someone who does. It does take practice and time in order to achieve these things. Influential aspects in life can be done by someone on a momentary basis or they can be done during the long term in someone's life. If you want to be of influence to someone you'll need to use your inner abilities and qualities and be a persistent, perseverant person. If you want to be of influence and get people to like you or want to be around you, you will need to use your charismatic and energetic qualities to be a better person socially and be able to win others over to your favor.

Chapter 9

The Art Of Social Interaction

Social interaction is not an easy feat to accomplish for many. It takes determination, perseverance, dedication, great communication skills and a lot of effort. Many people will want to take the easy way out and not allow the concept of seeking an effective or intricate means of social communication but only something that seems simple or effective enough to do the task at hand.

The concept of the art of social interaction exists in our world in every interaction we partake in. We are in a constant state of social communication and speaking to others in some form whether it be our jobs, families, group settings, friends, and a plethora of other scenarios. Social interaction is an intricate and imperative part of our world and tackling the idea of it is something that many people may not fully understand because most people don't tend to think of the minor intricacies by which they communicate, their reasons for communicating socially and simply just participate in the act without much introspection.

The art of social interaction is the beautiful concept of being able to master the wonderful nature of interacting with others and becoming a master at this very concept and being able to speak to others with grace, eloquence, and ease and being in control of the situation at hand.

Social interaction is a concept that should be understood, studied and examined by every person out there in some form for them to better understand their own actions, intentions and behaviors in given social situations, and for ways a person can better improve their situation in a social setting or when interacting with others. Yet, it's rare that people actually worry about their own social interactions with others or the methods they use to communicate with others. People tend to not study or worry about the methods and means by which they interact with others and as a result, they never improve their social skills and stay in the same situation they have been in.

For many people this may not be a bad thing, for interacting with family is different than interacting with a boss or co-worker, and they seem to 'get by' in the situation, however, for others they can truly use the benefits of introspection and further understanding their roles and behaviors in social situations and scenarios.

Social interaction is one of the most important aspects a person can experience in their daily life and should be encouraged to improve and understand in order for a person to further their life and grow in different social areas. Maybe your social interaction with others is stunting your life in different forms and you're just not getting what you want out of life, or the right people to come into your life. This is why it is important for you as a person to learn your social behaviors and become an expert in the concept of social interaction so you can improve your life socially and gain and win the people in your life that will better you in many forms, influence your life in a positive way and help you grow overall.

It is imperative that in order to display great social skills you utilize the power of displaying your intellect and eloquence through the art of spoken word, social interaction and the concept of expressing yourself in various forms. You must learn to use your intellect, talents, abilities and gifts to express yourself in different manners and forms and through the gift of charisma and being able to showcase these different talents.

Ways to improve your social skills include:

Positive body language: Exuding positive body language can assist a person in building their social skills and to appear and seem more approachable to others. Maintain good posture and have good eye contact with people you're speaking to.

Initiate conversations: Learn to initiate conversations with others, rather than being the passive person on the side who rarely talks or just agrees or speaks with someone rather than takes the proactive step. Use open-ended questions to establish deeper and more meaningful dialogue and conversation and find common ground to establish rapport

Be a good listener: Be a good listener and someone who shows interest and enthusiasm. It's important to show an interest in the other person and their situation and to focus on the other person rather than not showing an interest or not being a very good listener. Nod often and summarize key points to show an active interest in the situation.

Display empathy: It's a good idea to display empathy towards someone in a social interaction or situation. This way, you can show that you care about their situation and have a genuine interest and sympathy for what they are conversing about. Respond with sympathy and show concern rather than not caring about the situation or showing a lack of interest.

Self-awareness: You will want to show a great amount of self-awareness and know what your strengths and weaknesses are in a social setting and situation. Possessing self-awareness allows you to become better socially and allows you to know yourself better so you can improve in your situation and be a better listener and social advocate in your life.

Speak articulately: It's a good idea to speak with articulation and precision and know the value of the words that are being spoken through you, rather than not understanding the concept of the importance of articulate speech. Speaking properly and articulately allows you to come across as an intelligent person and someone who knows what they are talking about, rather than someone who may not have an idea or who may not be as intelligent. Speaking in this manner allows you to display your intelligence in a brilliant way and it is imperative that you learn how to your voice to display your intellect in a social setting.

Give compliments: People enjoy being praised and compliments are a great way to break the ice. They can create positive energy for a given conversation and allow you something to even be able to talk about. This also allows you to show a genuine interest in the situation and the person.

Join a club or group: It's important to join clubs or groups where you can interact with and meet new and different people. This not only allows you to expand your social circle but allows you to practice your social skills with new situations and different people. Find groups and clubs that are related to interests and activities you enjoy.

Use your intellect: Use and display your intellect in social situations. You'll want to show-off your intellect and display to others that you are a sharp, capable, intelligent, charismatic person who has the ability to interact with social precision, talent and confidence. This will help you achieve the results you desire.

Practice often: Practicing often allows you to improve your social skills immensely and by putting yourself in social situations where you can have small talk with new people, different people, and allows you to hone your social skills in general. If you get the chance to practice socializing many times a day, you'll be making progress than if you only had occasional interactions.

Step out of your comfort zone: Growth often happens when you come out of your comfort zone and decide to take on new challenges and endeavors. Challenge yourself to engage in social events that are out of your regular boundaries. Join new events, go to different group meetups and local events, and participate in community or volunteer activities. By attending new social events and experiences, you'll step out of your comfort zone and have a greater confidence in socializing.

The concept of public speaking

Many people tend to fear the concept of public speaking or feel as if it's a difficult thing to do. They get nervous or scared at the idea of being in front of so many different people and having to be the center of attention or projecting their voice to others or being the only person speaking at a large event.

Public speaking is not a scary or horrifying situation where a person is situated in the midst of a grueling audience they have to entertain for a specific period of time, and where they are the center of attention or what it seems to be. Many people tend to not always want to be the center of attention as well, which is where the concept seems very difficult or something that is not simple for many people to do.

Public speaking is not what a person may seem to be. It is not a concept that should be perceived as difficult, scary, nerve wrecking or any of the above. It in fact needs to be perceived differently by others. The concept of public speaking is one where a person, you, can relay your opinions, values and beliefs to others and is a great and amazing opportunity for you to have a huge and special magnetic and amazing effect on others in a hugely positive way. It is in fact a great and beautiful, intriguing blessing that a person can undergo and experience and is a great opportunity for a person to be of magnificent influence to others.

Being a public speaker can allow a person to have a wonderful and great influence on a large number of people and can allow a person to become an inspiration to others through many different means and forms. The idea of being a public speaker can further allow a person to be of great influence on others and use their charisma and persuasive abilities and skills to aid and benefit others and to relay their own messages and ideas to the masses in order to help others grow and to change lives in a very positive and beneficial way. It can be a monumental way to showcase someone's social and speaking skills and is a very beneficial way to be able to influence others on a grand scale.

Chapter 10

Being Perseverant As An Influential Person

Perseverance is noted for being a great way to success and it's about achieving someone's goals despite having challenges in the situation. It is the ability to come through in the face of anything difficult, while being focus and determined. It actually paves the way for many accomplishments.

Perseverance is a great driving force that allows people to achieve their dreams and lets someone strive through. Perseverance is a wonderful determination that lets people to continue moving forward and lets people stay focused on their long-term objectives.

Perseverance is a feat that allows for personal growth and lets a person push through adversity and lets someone achieve their goals and pull through.

Perseverance is a quality that can help people influence others and achieve their goals. It's the ability to keep going when things get difficult or when there are delays in achieving success. Perseverance can be developed and is not a personality trait. Here are some ways to influence perseverance and how it can help with success:

- Learn: Learning can help influence perseverance.
- Peer pressure: Peer pressure can have an impact on perseverance, but it's not long-lasting.
- Chat with a successful peer: Talking with a successful peer can be encouraging or discouraging.
- Set milestones: Break down goals into small, attainable milestones.
- Make progress visible: Make progress visible to yourself.
- Reflect: Engage in reflective practice.
- Capture small successes: Celebrate small successes as you go.
- Review: Continuously review what you're doing and how you're achieving your goals.
- Be courageous together: Being courageous together can make work and people stronger.

Perseverance is a very important and wonderful quality for a person to have. In order to be perseverant, a person must be a very determined, hard-working person who seeks to be diligent in all they do and lives their life in a specific way.

A perseverant person is one who moves forward and pushes through despite adversity and other problems and is diligent with the things they do for others. In order to be a persuasive and influential person you will want to harness perseverance and allow it to be exposed in your life and seep out to your world and showcase it by being enthusiastic about the situation.

A perseverant person learns how to break down their goals into manageable ones and can easily attain their goals and be successful at what they do. They utilize their knowledge and ideas and their persistence to be able to accomplish or achieve what they need in life.

To be a person of influence and to know how to use your talents or gifts to teach others how to influence others, you will want to attain the quality of perseverance, for no matter what the outcome, you will always come through due to the diligence you possess within.

Do you know of people who have this quality, or do you have this quality yourself? Have you ever tried to develop this trait and use it to get what you wanted or needed in life?

If you've tried to develop this trait, you probably will have found out that it takes time and abilities to be able to develop it in any form and it's not something that is done overnight. Determination and using it in different forms allows the concept of perseverance to develop more and further and allows someone to be able to utilize this ability and do the best they can with it and become a better person overall.

Perseverance and influence

How does being of influence relate to perseverance? You may wonder how being of influence and gaining people to trust or like you or winning people's hearts over can relate to being a perseverant person? It only does through the notion that in order to get what you want, you will have to struggle through and gain the things that you so desire that are needed in your life through hard work, dedication and striving through which is the hallmark of what being a perseverant person is.

You might be in a social setting trying to get people's attention or trying to get people to like you, and the best way to utilize your situation to your advantage is to work through any challenges that may be occurring in order to gain the strength you need and the momentum you need to get the things that you want in the given situation.

Perseverance can assist a person greatly when it comes to being a more influential person in general and can help with many different facets and areas in life. It can help you learn how to utilize other abilities you may have in order to become a better person and better be able to harness these abilities.

Studies have shown that those who fail and overcome failures can actually become more perseverant people in general and can succeed in greater ways in the long run. Further studies have shown that individuals who have faced and experienced failures of different kinds generally develop a stronger resolve and an increased capacity to persevere. This is because overcoming challenges builds resilience and can teach a person valuable lessons which can help them with having success in their future.

Other studies tried to show that experiencing negative emotions in the face of challenges will diminish perseverance towards someone's goals. On the other hand, positive emotions tended to enhance perseverance. So, encountering a setback leads to frustration and anger and can in turn hinder or stop decision-making and the ability to solve problems. The anger that is developed as a result of the frustration can become too much to deal with, so a person then ends up abandoning the goal as a result.

The ways to build perseverance skills

Set achievable goals

Set realistic and achievable goals to foster perseverance in a very effective manner. You will want to break down larger objectives into smaller manageable tasks and maintain a sense of progress. Success in smaller tasks builds confidence for much larger challenges and allows a person to be able to foster a sense of success and independence.

Develop a growth mindset

Develop a mindset that will want you to grow as a person and become better in the aspects you partake in and allow you to be a better person in general. Once you develop this kind of state of mind, you can further enhance your mental state and be a better person in general. Live your life with the state of mind that you seek to grow and further yourself in life and pursue your goals, rather than remaining stagnant in a given field or situation.

Learn from failure

Adopt a positive attitude towards different failures and you will need to view failures as opportunities rather than negative situations that have happened to you. Educational psychology suggests that reflecting on what went wrong in a failed attempt and devising new strategies enhances the ability to persevere and move past the situation into a brighter and newer situation and future.

Build resilience

Resilience, the capability to recover from difficulties, is very closely linked to perseverance. Techniques such as mindfulness, stress management, and emotional regulation, as studied in positive psychology, can help build resilience and can help a person develop perseverance and become a stronger person overall.

Adopt an attitude of acceptance

Developing a willingness to remain in contact with unhelpful internal experiences; thoughts, memories, emotions, bodily sensations, as we encounter obstacles and challenges is paramount to perseverance. Mindfulness and coping style coaching can aid in adopting an attitude of acceptance. You will want to have an attitude of acceptance towards various attitudes and feelings in life. This will allow you to develop different types of perseverance and let it grow within your body, mind and soul and help you to become a stronger person overall.

How to use perseverance practically and in social settings

Perseverance can be used practically and in social settings. A person can use it to harness good outcomes and attitudes for themselves and can use the concept of perseverance to gain friends and win the attitudes of people over and can do it using a greater personality and to enhance their personality and their own selves.

Being a perseverant person in social settings and to exude confidence and create a better personality for someone can help with their social situations and can help someone over social issues such as social anxiety or agoraphobia or different kinds of phobias.

It allows a person to develop and gain confidence to overcome these kinds of phobias or issues and lets a person heal naturally and learn to overcome these kinds of feelings and situations.

If you're hanging out with friends- you can be yourself and have fun and be doing well in a social setting but there might be a setback and what you can do during this situation is use your skills of perseverance to push through the situation and not let it affect you for you should know that you're a better person because of any negative situations that occur to you and that you can overcome them and not let them ruin or affect your life.

If you're trying to give a speech or influence others, then you can use key of perseverance to push through and give the wonderful speech of yours and allow yourself to be of influence to others and not allow any nervousness you may have or anything to hold or set you back. This wonderful characteristic can be of great help to you or to others in many given settings and can allow and help you during times of crisis or during other times in your life when situations seem too difficult to deal with.

Perseverance is a beautiful aspect that can assist a person with becoming a better socialite, elevating their social skills and helping a person with how to influence people on better and higher levels.

Being able to win friends and influence people is an important feat that people may think about but not yet aspire to do due to the difficulty involved and not knowing exactly how to elevate your social skills, your charisma and take it to the next level. However, there are methods and tactics that a person can use in order to enhance their lives and let their influence be of impact to others and be the influential and charismatic person they desire to be and were meant to be.

Being of influence takes persistence, perseverance, charisma, passion and many other qualities that need to be put together in order for a person to harbor this situation and be able to do what they need to do in order to reach the desired statistics and situation they want to be in. Getting people to like you takes amazing social skills and is an art along with the beauty of persuasion. If you want to persuade people to do what you want, then you will want to get them to like you and have to be a very likable person, charismatic, master the art of persuasion and encompass a variety of other qualities in order to get the desired results you need. Influencing others means doing so under the guise of being extremely positive and beneficial for everyone and being a decent and good person under the pretense of good morality.

Being a socially confident person takes time, effort, charisma and practice. With enough of these qualities, you can learn the art of social interaction and gain more friends and learn the art of influencing others in your life and be a great inspiration to others as well.

www.ingramcontent.com/pod-product-compliance
Lightning Source LLC
LaVergne TN
LVHW010410070526
838199LV00065B/5939